About Skill Builders Phonics

by Deborah and Larry Morris

Welcome to Rainbow Bridge Publishing's Skill Builders series. Like our Summer Bridge Activities™ collection, the Skill Builders series is designed to make learning both fun and rewarding.

The Skill Builders Phonics books are based on the premise that mastering language skills builds confidence and enhances a student's entire educational experience. A fundamental factor in learning to read is a strong phonics foundation, beginning with an awareness of the alphabet, understanding phonemic relationships and the concept of words, and moving onto word recognition.

Phonics Grade 1 contains pages on initial, ending, and medial consonants and moves on to vowels, word chunks, blends, digraphs, two-syllable words, compound words, and more.

A critical thinking section includes exercises to help develop higher-order thinking skills.

Learning is more effective when approached with an element of fun and enthusiasm—just as most children approach life. That's why the Skill Builders combine entertaining and academically sound exercises with eye-catching graphics and fun themes—to make reviewing basic skills at school or home fun and effective, for both you and your budding scholars.

Table of Contents

Initial Consonants

Print the beginning sound next to each picture.

Phonics Grade 1—RBP3438

A Trip to the Park
Print the beginning sound next to each picture.

Initial Consonants

Put an X on the picture that does not belong. Write its beginning sound on the line.
Trace the whole word.

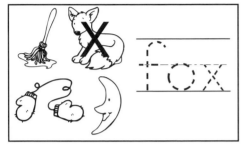

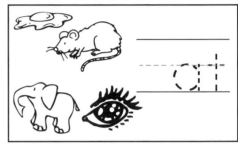

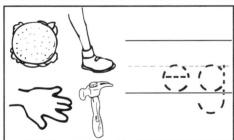

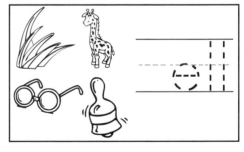

Draw one thing in the box that does not belong. Write its beginning sound below.

_____

_____

_____

Phonics Grade 1—RBP3438

Say the picture name. Circle the letter that begins each name. Print the capital letter below.

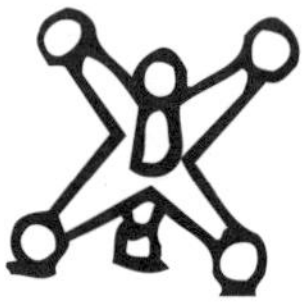

G
Q
J

J

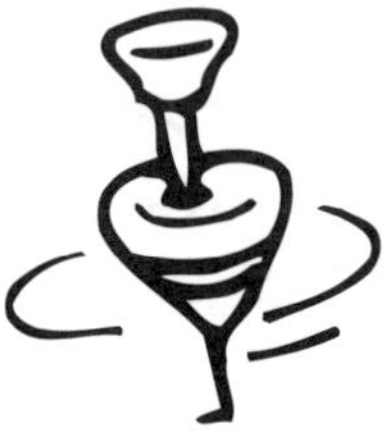

F
T
K

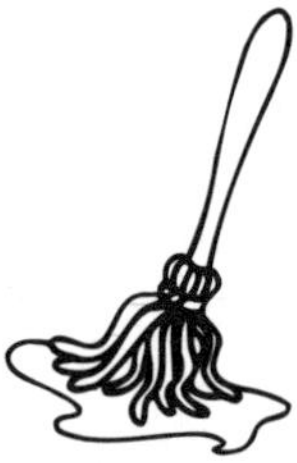

N
G
M

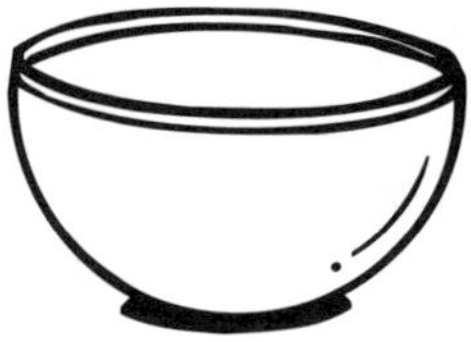

B
Z
D

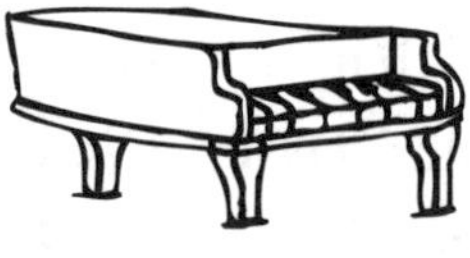

R
L
P

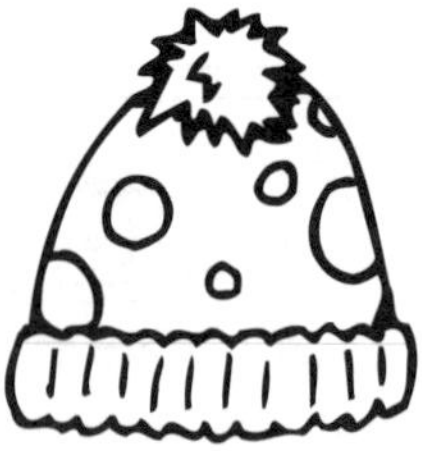

H
S
V

Rob's Room
Color all the things red that begin with the "r" sound. Color all the things blue that begin with the "b" sound.

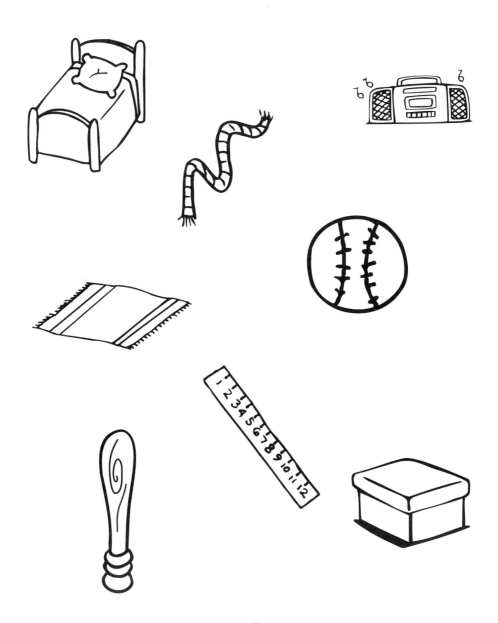

Phonics Grade 1—RBP3438

Initial Consonants

Say the name of each picture. Print the capital and small letters for the picture's beginning sound.

www.summerbridgeactivities.com

© Rainbow Bridge Publishing

Say the name of each picture. Print the ending sound.

 _____

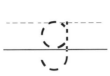 ___

 _____

 _____

 _____

 _____

 _____

Phonics Grade 1—RBP3438

Choose an ending sound from the letters in the center of the flower. Print the letter for each picture.

Final Consonants

Choose an ending sound from the Letter Box.
Print it below the picture with the same sound.

r	x	f	n
s	t	g	l

Phonics Grade 1—RBP3438

Final Consonants

Print the letter that makes the ending sound for each picture.

Final Consonants

Print the words from the Word Bank in the column with the same ending sound.

cat bag mug jet pen sun pot dog pin

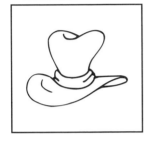

1. cat

1. _____

1. _____

2. _____

2. _____

2. _____

3. _____

3. _____

3. _____

Rob Reasons! Write a sentence using three words from the Word Bank. Remember to put a capital letter at the beginning and a period at the end of your sentence.

_____

_____

_____

© Rainbow Bridge Publishing   Phonics Grade 1—RBP3438

Beginning and Ending Consonants

Circle the beginning sound from the Letter Box. Circle the ending sound. Write each one next to the picture.

g	m
(b)	(k)
v	j

r	k
d	c
b	m

m	h
x	k
l	n

t	s
p	l
c	t

www.summerbridgeactivities.com   © Rainbow Bridge Publishing

Beginning and Ending Consonants

Circle the beginning sound from the Letter Box. Circle the ending sound. Write each one next to the picture.

s	k
r	g
d	v

r	g
d	k
z	m

l	n
t	r
v	c

m	j
b	v
p	s

© Rainbow Bridge Publishing Phonics Grade 1—RBP3438

Say the name of the picture. Underline its middle sound. Color the picture.

1.

j   <u>z</u>   d   l

2.

g   r   m   n

3.

m   h   d   t

4.

d   s   r   b

5.

f   g   t   b

Medial Consonants

Say the name of the picture. Underline its middle sound. Color the picture.

1.  d   p   l   h

2.  r   k   m   t

3.  t   p   z   n

4.  s   n   f   t

5.  m   p   l   d

Phonics Grade 1—RBP3438

Medial Consonants

Use the letters from the pond on page 19.
Print the middle sound for each picture under it.

Phonics Grade 1—RBP3438

Use the mixed-up letters to make a word. Write the word in the space.

In the **p e t** store, Rob saw a
_____ _____ _____
  t   e   p

___ ___ ___ ___ ___. It was in
 l   d   r   i   z   a

a ___ ___ ___ . A man had a ___ ___ ___ to
   o   x   b   u   g   b

feed the lizard. A ___ ___ ___ ___ ___ ___
                    n   k   i   e   t   t

had a ___ ___ ___ of ___ ___ ___ ___.
       u   p   c   k   l   i   m

"Mew, mew," the kitten said. "I like this!" It had

a ___ ___ ___ ___ ___ ___ on its neck.
   b   o   b   n   r   i

The ribbon was blue. It had a ___ ___ ___,
                                        a   t   g

too. It said, "My name is ___ ___ ___ ___."
                           e   B   l   l

"How are you, kitten?"

___ ___ ___ asked.
b   R   o

Rob Reasons! Draw a picture of a pet you would like to have. Print a name for your pet. Use the sounds you hear to spell its name.

© Rainbow Bridge Publishing

Beginning, Ending, and Medial Consonants

Choose a letter from the balloons for each picture's beginning sound.

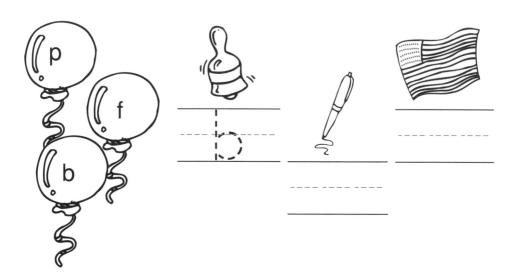

Choose a letter from the balloons for each picture's ending sound.

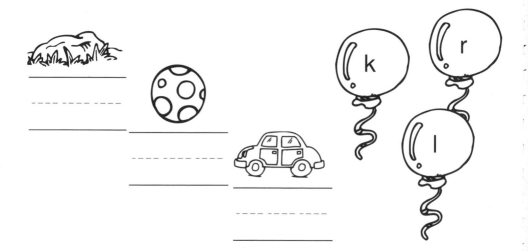

www.summerbridgeactivities.com

Beginning, Ending, and Medial Consonants

Choose a letter from the balloons for each picture's middle sound.

Choose a letter from the balloons to find the missing sounds.

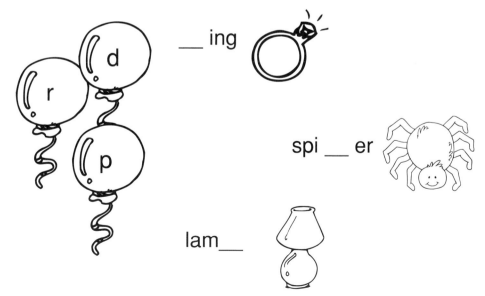

___ ing

spi ___ er

lam___

Phonics Grade 1—RBP3438

Draw a line to the name of the picture. Write a sentence using that word.

man

mop

map

_____

- -

_____

black

back

brick

_____

- -

_____

cup

cat

cab

_____

- -

_____

Draw a line to the name of the picture. Write a sentence using that word.

bat

back

bag

_____

- -

rap

ram

rim

_____

- -

snack

sap

snap

_____

- -

_____

Write the words from the Word Bank that rhyme with each bird's name.

black	rat	plan	back	bat
man	van	flat	track	

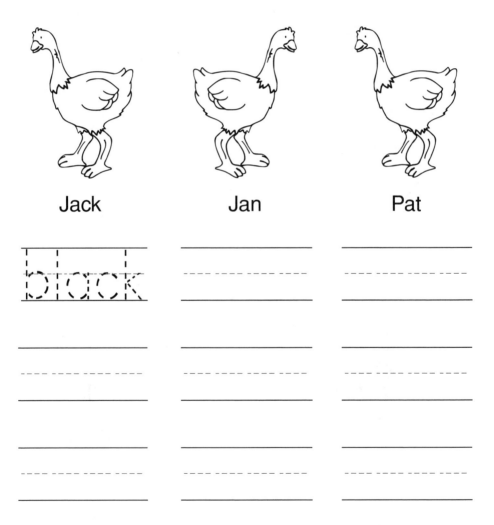

Jack   Jan   Pat

black

Short Vowels: a

Write the words from the Word Bank that rhyme with each bird's name.

sad	jam	wax	fax	ham
ram	had	ax	mad	

Tad   Sam   Max

© Rainbow Bridge Publishing   Phonics Grade 1—RBP3438

Short Vowels: i

Color in the dot by the word that names the picture.

- ⭘ win
- ⭘ wag
- 🔘 wig

- ⭘ mitt
- ⭘ mat
- ⭘ met

- ⭘ can
- ⭘ chin
- ⭘ kin

- ⭘ pill
- ⭘ pan
- ⭘ pin

- ⭘ laps
- ⭘ lips
- ⭘ lets

- ⭘ fit
- ⭘ fish
- ⭘ fat

Color in the dot by the word that names the picture.

○ mix	○ win	○ kit
○ fix	○ twins	○ kick
○ six	○ tan	○ sick

○ dig	○ pig	○ lip
○ dip	○ twig	○ lid
○ dish	○ jig	○ led

Phonics Grade 1—RBP3438

Short Vowels: i

For each box, find three rhyming words in a row. They can go across, up, down, or on a diagonal. Color the three squares.

twig	tin	wit
fin	fig	win
dig	sit	pig

pin	lick	hill
chin	pill	hit
fill	pick	pit

wig	brick	tip
him	trick	sit
hip	tick	lip

thick	sick	fin
spin	skin	twin
stick	fib	did

Rob Reasons! Find the four words that are parts of your body. Write them.

__ __ __ __   __ __ __

__ __ __   __ __ __

Change the first letter in each word to make a new word. Choose a letter from the box. Write the new word.

hot
p s t

p o t

top
r p s

____ ____ ____

cob
p r d

____ ____ ____

box
f w r

____ ____ ____

not
s g b

____ ____ ____

hop
r t g

____ ____ ____

bob
d g w

____ ____ ____

rock
l g b

____ ____ ____ ____

Phonics Grade 1—RBP3438

Change the last letter in each word to make a new word. Choose a letter from the box. Write the new word.

dog
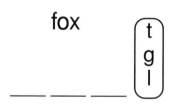

d   o   t
___ ___ ___

lot
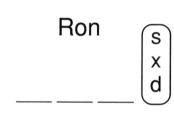

___ ___ ___

fox

t
g
l

___ ___ ___

Ron

s
x
d

___ ___ ___

mop

g
n
m

___ ___ ___

cot

m
v
p

___ ___ ___

not

g
d
m

___ ___ ___

slot

b
f
r

___ ___ ___ ___

Circle the short "e" words.

1. The (red)(sled) in the (shed) was a (mess)

2. Ned was sad when he saw it.

3. His pet Pepper had the sled for a bed.

4. Then Ned's mom had to sell the sled.

5. Ned and Pepper helped Mom fix the sled.

6. "Well, it looks better now," Mom said.

7. "Let's keep it then."

8. "Yes, it passes the test."

9. Next, Ted fed Pepper, who slept in a tent.

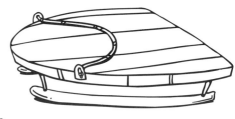

Phonics Grade 1—RBP3438

Short Vowels: e

Print a short "e" word from the story to finish each sentence.

"Did you get all the eggs?"
the hen asked from her nest.
"I like the green and the blue,
but the red ones are best."

The rabbit set them in his basket.
Then he went away fast,
before Hen could ask it,
"Where are you going?"

1. Rabbit got the ___ ___ ___ ___.

2. The ___ ___ ___ eggs were the

  ___ ___ ___ ___ ones.

3. Rabbit ___ ___ ___ them into his basket.

4. He ___ ___ ___ ___ away fast.

  Rob Reasons! Where do you think the rabbit went?

www.summerbridgeactivities.com

Choose any word from the Word Bank to make a silly story.

1. I found a ___ ___ ___ ___ ___.

skunk
slug
truck

2. I put it in my ___ ___ ___ ___.

mug
hut
junk

3. My mom gave it a ___ ___ ___.

hug
bun
bus

4. Then it ate a ___ ___ ___ ___.

bug
cub
duck

These words end in "at" and "an."

Write the word after the picture. Then color the pictures.

> | hat | pan | cat | man |
> |-----|-----|-----|-----|
> | mat | can | van | ran |

 My c   a   t sat on a big

 ___ ___ ___.

Dan was a nice  ___ ___ ___.

He had a blue  ___ ___ ___.

He had a new ___ ___ ___.

Use the words from the Word Bank on page 36.

Dan put a little ___ ___ ___ and a

big ___ ___ ___ in his blue van.

My cat  ___ ___ ___ to Dan; it

ran fast.

The cat sat in the  ___ ___ ___.

The silly cat sat on Dan's  ___ ___ ___.

Then the cat went to sleep.

Phonics Grade 1—RBP3438

Say the picture word. Circle the word that goes with the picture. Then color the pictures.

(map)

tap

snap

snap

clap

map

lap

map

tap

tack

rack

pack

track

back

jack

sack

black

back

Chunks: it, ig

Circle the words that sound the same.

hit   cat   fit   sit   pan   bit

map   kit   rack   pit   mitt   dad

Say the picture and write the word.

— — —   — — — —   — — —

Circle words that sound like <u>big</u>. Put an X over the words that sound like <u>fit</u>.

dig   kit   can   sit   jig   pat

© Rainbow Bridge Publishing   Phonics Grade 1—RBP3438

Rob Wins!
Find out what happens to Rob by saying the picture and writing the word next to it.

kick	chin	shin
stick	brick	spin

Rob likes to 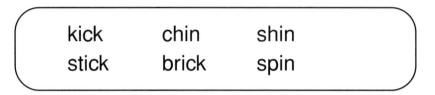 k i c k

his ball. He kicks it far. But one day he tripped on

a _____ _____ _____ _____ _____ and fell

on a _____ _____ _____ _____ _____.

He hurt his _____ _____ _____ _____.

He hurt his  __ __ __ __.

The next day he played ball again. When he got

to 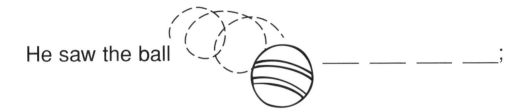 __ __ __ __, he kicked hard.

He saw the ball 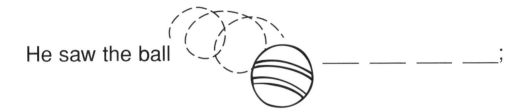 __ __ __ __;

he saw it go in the net.

"Good __ __ __ __," his

friends said. "Rob, you win!"

 Phonics Grade 1—RBP3438

Solve the riddles by using words from the box.

pot	knot	lock	clock	shot	sock

When you tie a rope, it's called a k n o t .

You put the pan with the ___ ___ ___.

Before she put on her shoe, she put on her

___ ___ ___ ___.

I went to the doctor and got a ___ ___ ___ ___.

You open this with a key. ___ ___ ___ ___

It has hands, but it is not a person. It's a

___ ___ ___ ___ ___.

Across

1. You use it to clean the floor.
4. Rabbits __ __ __ from place to place.
5. You cook with it.

Down

2. The sound you hear when you stick a balloon with a pin.
3. Not the bottom, but the __ __ __.
4. Not cold, but __ __ __.

Phonics Grade 1—RBP3438

Say the picture word. Circle the word that goes with the picture. Then color the pictures.

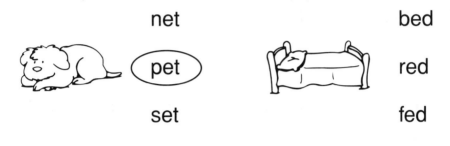

net

pet

set

bed

red

fed

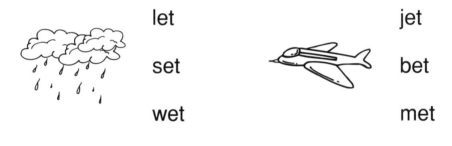

let

set

wet

jet

bet

met

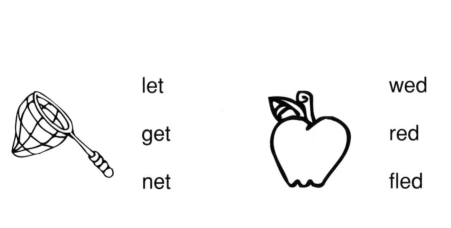

let

get

net

wed

red

fled

Chunks: en, ell

Circle the words that sound the same.

ten	hot	hen	pen
pig	kit	hop	men
tan	den	tack	then

Say the picture and write the word.

___ ___ ___ ___   ___ ___ ___ ___

___ ___ ___ ___ ___

     Phonics Grade 1—RBP3438

Say the picture word and draw a line from the picture to the word.

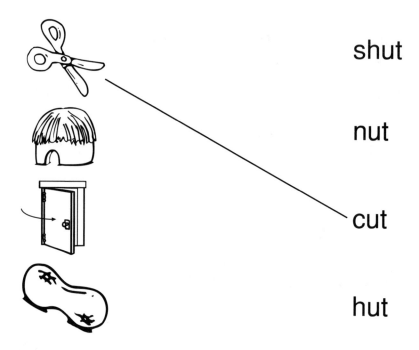

shut

nut

cut

hut

Read and say the words in the box. Then write the words that sound like <u>bug</u>.

| dug | men | tug | pen | plug |

_____   _____   _____

- - - - - - - - - - -   - - - - - - - - - - -   - - - - - - - - - - -

_____   _____   _____

Chunks: un, uck

For each picture, add a letter from the Letter Box to make a word.

| s | z | p | b | r |

___**s**_ un

___un

___un

| tr | l | d | cl | br |

___uck

___uck

___uck

© Rainbow Bridge Publishing   Phonics Grade 1—RBP3438

Read the words in the list. Search for each word in the puzzle. Circle the whole word.

1. brick	6. sack
2. shut	7. truck
3. plan	8. twig
4. rock	9. less
5. shell	10. stop

```
w  b  c  c  t  w  i  g  k  l
l  x  s  t  o  p  v  z  c  a
g  k  a  z  z  h  a  j  i  n
k  c  v  k  t  v  x  h  r  a
o  a  e  a  x  v  b  t  b  l
b  s  f  k  h  z  u  e  k  p
s  q  l  s  c  h  m  h  f  g
l  l  e  h  s  u  q  c  i  i
k  i  s  r  f  e  r  c  s  w
e  k  c  o  r  m  l  t  m  d
```

www.summerbridgeactivities.com

Fill in the correct dot for each sentence.

1. A (green) tree frog has black skin.

       ○ true   ○ false

2. A green tree frog swims in a stream.

       ○ true   ○ false

3. Green tree frogs like to climb on tree trunks.

       ○ true   ○ false

Blend words combine two consonant sounds like <u>b</u> and <u>l</u> in <u>block</u>, or <u>g</u> and <u>r</u> in <u>grow</u>.

Circle all the blend words in the sentences about frogs. Write the words in these blanks.

1. green   2.

3.   4.

5.   6.

7.   8.

9.

    Phonics Grade 1—RBP3438

Blends

Print the word that answers each riddle. Then circle all the words with blends.

1. I am a (fruit.) I (grow) in bunches on (stems.) Sometimes I am (green)

___ ___ ___ ___ ___

2. I like to slide across the snow. I make brave kids scream and smile.

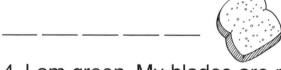

___ ___ ___ ___

3. I am made from grain. You can spread butter on a slice. Birds eat my crumbs.

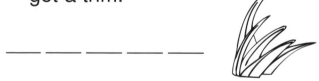

___ ___ ___ ___ ___

4. I am green. My blades are not sharp, but they get a trim.

___ ___ ___ ___ ___

5. I go slow on the grass and leave a trail.

___ ___ ___ ___ ___

www.summerbridgeactivities.com © Rainbow Bridge Publishing

Digraphs

A **digraph** is two consonants that together make a new sound, like <u>ch</u> or <u>sh</u>. Say the words <u>chip</u>, <u>show</u>, <u>when</u>, and <u>this</u>. Can you hear the digraphs?

Circle the digraphs in this poem.

I (ch)ose a (sh)ell upon the bea(ch).

When I put it to my ear

That shell went swish—

There was a fish!

Where did it go?

I did not know.

Into my shirt.

My brother cheered.

That fish I could not reach!

© Rainbow Bridge Publishing   Phonics Grade 1—RBP3438

Fill in the dot next to the correct word for each sentence.

1. Shelly and her mom like to _____.
   ◯ ship   ● shop

2. They _____ to go to the shoe store.
   ◯ chose   ◯ check

3. Shelly sat on the _____ to try shoes on.
   ◯ chimp   ◯ chair

4. "_____ do you like, Mom?"
   ◯ Which   ◯ When

5. "Those are not the right _____."
   ◯ dish   ◯ shade

6. She _____ the shoe box.
   ◯ shut   ◯ shell

7. "I like _____," said Shelly.
   ◯ then   ◯ these

Long Vowels

When a word has two vowels, the first one usually says its alphabet name, and the second is quiet. A vowel that says its name is called a **long vowel.**

For example: "make" says a long "a." The "e" is silent. Circle the words that have a long vowel.

 (blue)

 pail

 knot

 feet

 cake

 pin

 coat

 nine

Phonics Grade 1—RBP3438

Write the name of each picture.

Rob has a magic "E" hat. When he put in a

__c__ __a__ __n__ , he pulled out a

___ ___ ___ ___ . Next he put in

a ___ ___ ___ and pulled out a

___ ___ ___ ___ . When he put in

a ___ ___ ___ , he pulled out a

___ ___ ___ ___ . Last, he put in

a ___ ___ ___ and pulled out a

___ ___ ___ ___ .

Two-Syllable Words

Words have parts called **syllables.** Each syllable has one vowel sound. Read each word in the Word Bank. Circle each vowel you hear. Underline the two-syllable words. Then print the word next to its number in the story.

Word Bank			
1. seven	2. ribbon	3. kite	4. puppet
5. best	6. second	7. hello	8. yellow

I am (1) _____, and I am in (6) _____

grade. In class I made a (8) _____ and

green (3) _____. It had a (2)_____

for a tail. Mike made a kitten (4) _____. It

said "(7) _____" to me. I liked it the (5)

_____.

Write your own sentence using three or more of the words in the Word Bank.

_____

_____

_____

_____.

© Rainbow Bridge Publishing   Phonics Grade 1—RBP3438

Write the number of the sentence that tells about the picture in the space below. Then circle the two-syllable words.

1. The little kitten has eaten the button.

2. Open the oven and get the turkey.

3. My yellow jacket has a ticket in the pocket.

4. That number seven has on a ribbon.

-le Words

Read each word in the Word Bank. If it is something a turtle or people can do, print the word underneath the correct word. Some words will be under both.

Word Bank

wiggle	bubble	tickle	snuggle
paddle	buckle	giggle	whistle

turtle   people

_____   _____

_____   _____

_____   _____

                                    _____

                                    _____

                                    _____

                                    _____

                                    _____

Phonics Grade 1—RBP3438

Help finish the story. Print the number of the best word from the Word Bank in each blank. Read the story out loud.

Word Bank			
1. Cuddles	4. apple	7. beetles	10. candle
2. pickle	5. little	8. table	11. Pebbles
3. riddle	6. juggle	9. eagle	12. bottle

_____ saw an _____ up in its nest.

She was sitting at the _____ eating a red

_____. She wanted to put some fruit in the

nest. Her sister, _____, wanted to give it a

sweet _____. But I think it likes to eat

_____ best. So we put one in a glass

_____. I don't think it will see the bug. It is

too _____.

Compound Words

Can we have some fun? Let's take two words and make one! Use the underlined words to finish each riddle.

1. It is not a <u>horse</u> that can <u>fly</u>.

    It is a _____.

2. It is not the <u>sea</u> planted with <u>weeds</u>.

    It is _____.

3. It is not a <u>cup</u> filled with <u>cake</u>.

    It is a _____.

4. It is not a <u>pea</u> that is <u>nuts</u>.

    It is a _____.

Compound Words

Read each word in the Word Bank. If it is something to eat, write the number 1 in the space. If it is a place to go or something to ride, write the number 2 in the space. If you can play with it or make it, write the number 3 in the space.

Word Bank

a.	campground _____	b.	football _____
c.	airplane _____	d.	oatmeal _____
e.	baseball _____	f.	popcorn _____
g.	potpie _____	h.	snowman _____
i.	railroad _____	j.	sandbox _____

Write a story with three sentences. Use some of the compound words.

_____

_____

_____

_____

_____

_____

_____

_____

_____

Categories

Circle the word that does **not** answer the question.

1. What do you put on in the winter?

   pants   hat   mittens   boots   sandals

2. Which one can you have for a pet?

   mouse   spider   lion   goldfish   lizard

3. Which ones do we like to eat?

   cheese   pancakes   leaves   chicken   eggs

4. Where can you play?

   outside   street   sandbox   bedroom   slide

5. Which ones can our body do?

   huddle   run   float   fly   sleep

Phonics Grade 1—RBP3438

Categories

Read each list. Think what makes the words in the list alike. Pick a word from the Word Bank that names how the words are alike. Print the word in the blank.

1. rose
   buttercup
   pansy
   violet   _____

2. boots
   sandals
   loafers
   thongs   _____

3. milkshake
   soda
   juice
   hot chocolate   _____

4. kitten
   gerbil
   goldfish
   poodle   _____

5. orange
   yellow
   black
   green   _____

6. tired
   happy
   angry
   excited   _____

Word Bank
shoes
pets
colors
feelings
flowers
drinks

Making Inferences

Read each story. Then choose a word from the Word Bank to answer each question.

Word Bank
zoo garden birthday beach

1. Trina put on her swimsuit. Then she got her bucket. She put food in a basket. "Get a blanket and umbrella," Mom said.

Trina and her mom are going to the _____.

2. Max got the hoe. Next he dug in the dirt. Then he opened the packet of seeds and planted them. Last, he added some water.

Max is planting a _____.

3. Pam blew up the balloons. Kent got the cake and candles. Kristen picked up the presents. Nathan got the ice cream.

They are going to a _____ party.

4. First, Marta saw the monkeys. "Look, they swing from the branches!" "Give them a peanut through the bars," said Natalie.

Marta and Natalie are at the _____.

Phonics Grade 1—RBP3438

Making Inferences

Read each story. Write a sentence to answer the question.

1. Mom washed Jake's leg. Then she rubbed on some cream. Next, she put on a bandaid.

Why did Mom need cream and a bandaid?

_____

2. Jason turned on the lamp. He put on his pajamas. Then he brushed his teeth.

How can you tell it is night?

_____

3. Lori saw the clown blow up the balloon. The balloon got bigger and bigger. The clown poked it with a pin. Lori put her hands on her ears.

Why did Lori cover her ears?

_____

4. Katy reads a book with Jessy. Jessy likes to see the pictures. Katy tells Jessy when to turn the page.

How can you tell Katy is the big sister?

_____

Cause and Effect

Circle the word that will finish the sentence. Then write it in the blank.

1. If Jacob jumps in that puddle, he will get _____.

       hurt   wet   clean

2. Kylie missed the school bus, so she was _____.

       lost   late   tired

3. Mom got the stool because Juan is _____.

       tall   seven   little

4. The puppy got out because the gate was _____.

       locked   ugly   open

5. Our kite is up in the sky because the day is _____.

       rainy   windy   hot

Phonics Grade 1—RBP3438

Cause and Effect

Print the best ending from the Word Bank to finish each sentence.

Word Bank

it was cold outside   they got the prize
Tara's bike had a flat tire   we had to come inside
we could see the movie

1. Dad got the pump because

_____.

2. Our teacher pulled the shade so

_____.

3. It was time for bed, so

_____.

4. Jake turned on the heat because

_____.

5. Tammy's team won the game, so

_____.

Spider Spelling

1. Change the p in <u>pen</u> to t. ____ ____ ____

2. Change the n to d. ____ ____ ____

3. Change the t to l. ____ ____ ____

4. Change to d to t. ____ ____ ____

5. Change the l to w. ____ ____ ____

6. Change the t to b. ____ ____ ____

Draw a picture of the word you end up with.

Phonics Grade 1—RBP3438

Prediction

Circle the word that completes the pattern. Then write it in the blank.

1. a. grasshopper b. apple a. ant b. lemon a. _____
What comes next?

   green   banana   spider

2. a. hair b. pencil a. toe b. marker a._____
What comes next?

   leg   crayon   water

3. a. Spring b. cup a. Fall b. glass a. _____
What comes next?

   bottle   Winter   window

4. a. fork b. grass a. bowl b. leaf a. _____
What comes next?

   pea   gum   plate

5. a. dollar b. pizza a. penny b. pie a. _____
What comes next?

   dime   bank   money

www.summerbridgeactivities.com   © Rainbow Bridge Publishing

Prediction

Read each puzzle. Make an X on the blank by the best answer to each question.

Critical Thinking Skills

1. Kelly hits the baseball. It breaks the Millers' window. What will happen next?

_____ Mrs. Miller will give Kelly a new ball.

_____ Kelly will pay to fix the window.

_____ Nobody will find out the window is broken.

2. Baby Carter is sleeping. Landon slams the door. What will happen next?

_____The door will fall off.

_____Landon will go to sleep.

_____The baby will cry.

3. Clouds hide the sun. You can hear thunder. What will happen next?

_____Someone will scream.

_____It will get hot.

_____Rain will begin to fall.

4. Elliot finds a robin's egg. He puts it in the nest. What will happen next?

_____The egg will roll out of the nest.

_____A baby bird will hatch.

_____Elliot will take the nest home.

© Rainbow Bridge Publishing   Phonics Grade 1—RBP3438

Musical Rhymes

1. Make two sets of chunk words on 3 x 5 cards. You can use the following words or come up with your own. Put one word per card.

set	bell	bug	bun	buck	bat
net	dell	hug	fun	duck	cat
met	sell	jug	run	suck	hat
pet	tell	lug	sun	tuck	mat
get	well	mug	gun	luck	pat
bet	yell	rug			rat
jet	spell	tug			sat

cap	tick	bin	cot	dock
gap	kick	fin	dot	lock
lap	lick	kin	got	rock
map	sick	pin	hot	clock
nap	pick	sin	jot	sock
rap	quick	tin	not	
sap	trick	win	pot	

Musical Rhymes

2. Have children sit in a circle on the floor.

3. Display one set of cards on a wall chart, and put one set in the center of the circle face down. Put a star on the floor near the pile.

4. The first child picks a card from the pile and returns to his or her place on the floor.

5. The child reads the card out loud and thinks of a word that rhymes with the one on the card. The children are free to refer to the wall chart.

6. Play a musical tape as the children pass the card to the right. When the music stops, the child with the card repeats step 4. If a child cannot think of a word, he or she must put the card on the star in a second pile on the floor and sit out. The next child picks a card.

7. The game continues.

   You can play this with a classroom of children or with as few as two people with or without the music.

 **Spy**

Read the riddle. Write what you think it is about.

I am sailing in a ship
Upon the deep blue sea.
 spy this down below.
It is big as a bus, looking at us,
And spouting water at me.

What is it? _____

My grandmother has a locket.
It has no locks I see.
She keeps it in her pocket,
And away from me.
Sometimes she takes it out
And puts it on a shelf.
 spy it, and I open it. All by myself!

Write a sentence telling what you think
is in the locket.

_____

I have lost them, you see,
But they are not lost to me.
They are under my head on the bed.
If I lift up my pillow
 spy them, and uh-oh!
In their spot I find a dollar instead.

What are they? _____

Hidden Blends

Find the words in the Word Bank in the puzzle. Circle each word. Look for words that go across and down.

grape	spoon	drum	snack	trip
plant	clap	stick	free	brave
frog	price	smile	sleep	crab
straw				

```
s s g r a p e b c o
q n c y k g o r f p
o a w s p a l c p l
s c r s l g b t r a
t k b t m e h r i n
r n r i f k e i c t
a o a c r d l p e c
w o v k e r i z f r
n p e x e u m c g a
l s u x n m s k j b
```

On a piece of paper, write five sentences using words from the Word Bank. Remember to put a capital letter at the beginning of a sentence and a period or a question mark at the end.

Phonics Grade 1—RBP3438

Answer Pages

Page 3 — (Answers may be in either upper- or lowercase.)
R, L
F, D
N, S
J, B

Page 4
(Answers from left to right)
R, G, D, T, W

Page 5 — (Answers may be in either upper- or lowercase.)
F, M, C, R, L, B

Page 6
J, T, M, B, P, H

Page 7
Colored red: rug, ruler, radio, rope
Colored blue: bed, box, ball, bat

Page 8
(From left to right and top to bottom)
Zz, Ss, Xx
Ll, Ww, Gg
Cc, Nn

Page 9
g, l, p
t, n, r

Page 10 — (Answers rotate clockwise.)
k, b, x, d, s

Page 11 — (Answers rotate clockwise.)
t, g, s, n, f, r

Page 12
t, g, g, t, n, n, t
g, n

Page 13
cat	pin	mug
jet	pen	dog
pot	sun	bag

Page 14
b, k
d, m
m, n
t, l

Page 15
s, g
r, k
l, r
m, s

Page 16
| **1.** z | **2.** g | **3.** m |
| **4.** b | **5.** g | |

Page 17
| **6.** d | **7.** t | **8.** n |
| **9.** s | **10.** l | |

Page 18
m, d, l
b, p, r
g, n, t

Page 20
pet, lizard, box, bug, kitten, cup, milk, ribbon

www.summerbridgeactivities.com

Answer Pages

Page 21
tag, Bell, Rob

Page 22 — (Answers are from left to right, top to bottom.)
b, p, f
k, l, r

Page 23 — (Answers from left to right)
g, d, t
r, d, p

Page 24
map
black
cab
Sentence answers will vary.

Page 25
bat
ram
snap
Sentence answers will vary.

Page 26

black	man	rat
track	plan	bat
back	van	flat

Page 27

sad	ram	wax
had	ham	fax
mad	jam	ax

Page 28

wig	mitt	chin
pin	lips	fish

Page 29

six	twins	sick
dish	pig	lid

Page 30 — (Answers are from left square to right, or top to bottom. Squares colored are the words listed.)

twig	fill
fig	pill
pig	hill

brick	spin
trick	skin
tick	twin

Rob Reasons: chin, hip, lip, skin

Page 31

p	p
r	f
g	t
g	l

Page 32

t	g
g	d
m	p
d	b

Page 33
1. red, sled, shed, mess
2. Ned, when
3. pet, Pepper, sled, bed
4. Then, Ned's, sell, sled
5. Ned, Pepper, helped, sled
6. Well, better (said)
7. Let's, then
8. Yes, test (passes)
9. Next, Ted, fed, Pepper, slept, tent

Page 34
1. eggs   2. red, best
3. set   4. went
Rob Reasons: Answers will vary.

© Rainbow Bridge Publishing   Phonics Grade 1—RBP3438

Answer Pages

Page 35
Answers will vary.

Page 36
cat, mat
man
van
hat

Page 37
can, pan
ran
van
hat

Page 38 — (Answers from left to right)
map, clap
lap, pack
track, sack

Page 39
hit, fit, sit, bit
kit, pit, mitt
pig, twig, wig
dig, jig
~~kit~~, ~~sit~~

Page 40
kick
stick
brick
chin

Page 41
shin
kick
spin
kick

Page 42
knot
pot
sock
shot
lock
clock

Page 43
Across

1. mop	**4.** hop	**5.** pot

Down

2. pop	**3.** top	**4.** hot

Page 44
(Answers are left to right, top to bottom.)
pet, bed
wet, jet
net, red

Page 45
ten, hen, pen
men, den, then
bell, shell, well

Page 46

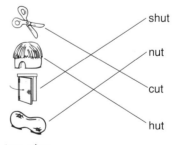

shut
nut
cut
hut

dug, tug, plug

Page 47

s	r	b
d	l	tr

Answer Pages

Page 48

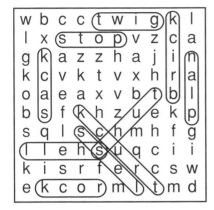

Page 49
1. F   **2.** F   **3.** T

1. green   **2.** tree   **3.** frog
4. black   **5.** skin   **6.** swims
7. stream   **8.** climb   **9.** trunks

Page 50
1. grapes
2. sled
3. bread
4. grass
5. snail

Page 51
chose, shell, beach
When
That, shell, swish
there, fish
Where
shirt
brother, cheered
That, fish, reach

Page 52
1. shop   **2.** chose   **3.** chair
4. Which   **5.** shade   **6.** shut
7. these

Page 53
(Answers are left to right, top to bottom.)
blue, pail
feet
cake
coat, nine

Page 54
can, cane, tub, tube, pin, pine, man, mane

Page 55
1. seven   6. second   8. yellow
3. kite   2. ribbon   4. puppet
7. hello   5. best
Sentences will vary.

Page 56
1, 3, 4, 2
1. little, kitten, eaten, button
2. open, oven, turkey
3. yellow, jacket, ticket, pocket
4. number, seven, ribbon

Page 57
Turtle: wiggle, paddle, bubble
People: wiggle, paddle, bubble, buckle,
             tickle, snuggle, giggle, whistle

Page 58
1 or 11; 9; 8; 4; 1 or 11; 2; 7; 12; 5

Page 59
1. horsefly   **2.** seaweed
3. cupcake   **4.** peanut

© Rainbow Bridge Publishing   Phonics Grade 1—RBP3438

Answer Pages

Page 60
a. 2 **b.** 3 **c.** 2 **d.** 1, 3 **e.** 3
f. 1, 3 **g.** 1, 3 **h.** 3 **i.** 2 **j.** 3

Page 61
1. sandals **2.** lion **3.** leaves
4. street **5.** fly

Page 62
1. flowers **2.** shoes **3.** drinks
4. pets **5.** colors **6.** feelings

Page 63
1. beach **2.** garden **3.** birthday **4.** zoo

Page 64
Answers will vary.
1. Jake had hurt his leg.
2. Jason is getting ready for bed.
3. When a balloon pops, it makes a loud noise.
4. Katy can read and knows when to turn the pages.

Page 65
1. wet **2.** late **3.** little
4. open **5.** windy

Page 66
1. Tara's bike had a flat tire
2. we could see the movie
3. we had to come inside
4. it was cold outside
5. they got the prize

Page 67
1. ten **2.** Ted **3.** led
4. let **5.** wet **6.** web
Picture: spiderweb

Page 68
1. spider **2.** leg **3.** Winter
4. plate **5.** dime

Page 69
1. Kelly will pay to fix the window.
2. The baby will cry.
3. Rain will begin to fall.
4. A baby bird will hatch.

Page 72
whale
Answers will vary.
teeth

Page 73

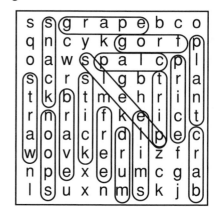

rat ă	ape ā	snail ā	crayfish ā
bear b	cat c	centipede s	cheetah ch
deer d	elephant ĕ	seal ē	bee ē
fish f	gorilla g	giraffe j	horse h
inchworm ĭ	crocodile ī	jaguar j	kangaroo k
lion l	mouse m	newt n	gong ng

Phonics Grade 1—RBP3438

Sounds and Letters Chart

dŏg ŏ	goat ō	stone ō	goose ū
wood o͞o	crow ō	pig p	quail kw
rabbit r	skunk s	shark sh	turtle t
thrust th	duck ŭ	Duke ū	vulture v
wolf w	whale wh	fox x	xylophone z
yak y	fly ī	pony ē	zebra z

© Rainbow Bridge Publishing